INFOMOJIS

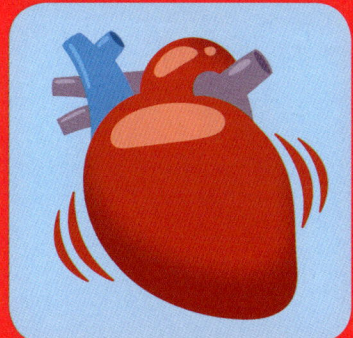
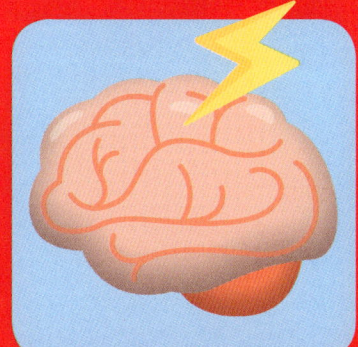

HUMAN BODY

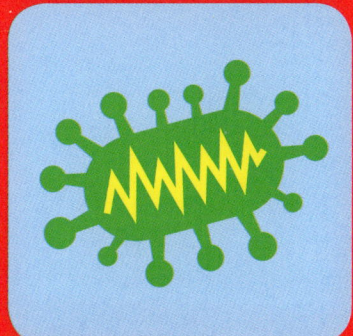
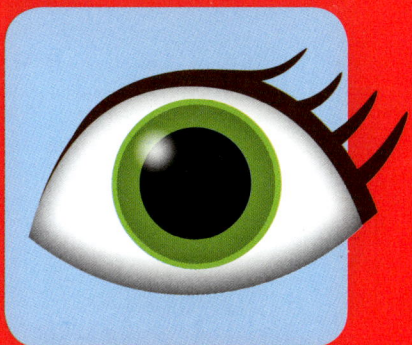

First published in paperback in
Great Britain in 2021 by Wayland
Copyright © Hodder and Stoughton, 2018
All rights reserved

Executive editor: Adrian Cole
Produced by Tall Tree Ltd
Editor: Jon Richards
Designer: Ed Simkins

ISBN: 978 1 5263 0692 0

Wayland
An imprint of Hachette Children's Group
Part of Hodder and Stoughton
Carmelite House
50 Victoria Embankment
London EC4Y 0DZ

An Hachette UK Company
www.hachette.co.uk
www.hachettechildrens.co.uk

Printed and bound in Dubai

MIX
Paper from
responsible sources
FSC® C104740
FSC
www.fsc.org

THE BODY'S STRUCTURE

Cell

Your body is an amazing collection of trillions of tiny structures called cells. These cells join together to form tissues and organs which carry out the complicated jobs that keep you alive.

From cells to systems

Cells
A cell is the smallest independent unit in the human body.

The biggest cell in the body is the ovum, or egg, found in women. It measures about 0.1 mm across.

Tissues
Similar cells join together to form tissues that carry out specific jobs.

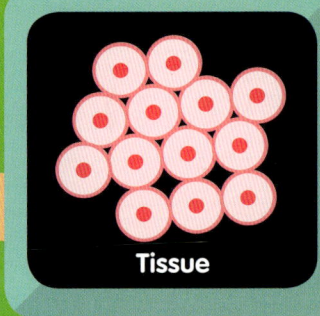
Tissue

Ovum (x5)

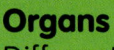

Organs
Different tissues join together to form organs, such as the liver and heart.

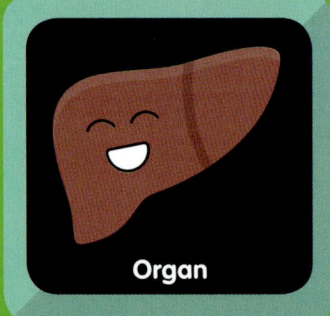
Organ

Q: How many cells are there in a human body?

A: Numbers vary, but estimates say that there may be about **37.2 trillion** cells in a body.

The longest cells in the body are the nerve cells in the leg, which run from the base of the spine to the foot.

A: Other estimates say that there are 10 bacteria cells in the human gut for every cell in a human body.

The largest internal organ is the liver, which can weigh about **1.5 kg.**

Medical marvel
In the ancient world, much of the body's workings (including how it got ill), were believed to be the work of the gods. That was until people like me, Hippocrates (c.460–c.370 BCE), put together some of the first books on anatomy and medicine.

The body's biggest organ is the skin, which can weigh about 3.5 kg.

HIPPOCRATES

Systems
Whole body systems are made from tissues and organs and carry out large-scale roles within the body.

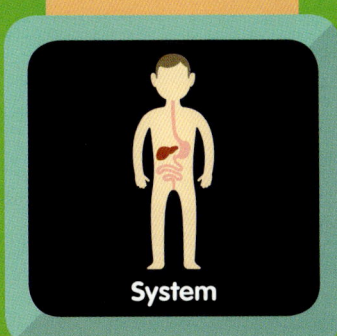

System

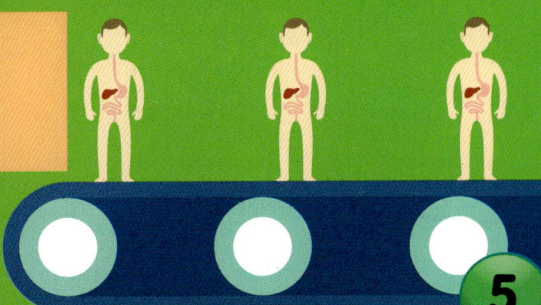

SKIN, HAIR AND NAILS

Surrounding your body, the skin does so much more than just hold everything together. It helps to keep you cool and warm, and offers the first barrier in the fight against attack from the outside world.

Skin structure

Epidermis

Dermis

The top layer is called the epidermis. It is made from hard, dead skin cells that are filled with a tough substance called keratin.

Touch sensor

Beneath the epidermis is the dermis. This contains touch sensors so you can feel heat and cold, pressure and pain.

Blood vessels carry oxygen and nutrients to the skin cells.

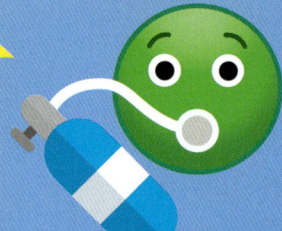

Blood vessel

Your feet have about **250,000** sweat glands on them. Bacteria break down this sweat, which is why your feet can sometimes be extra smelly!

Sweat glands produce a liquid called sweat.

Sweat gland

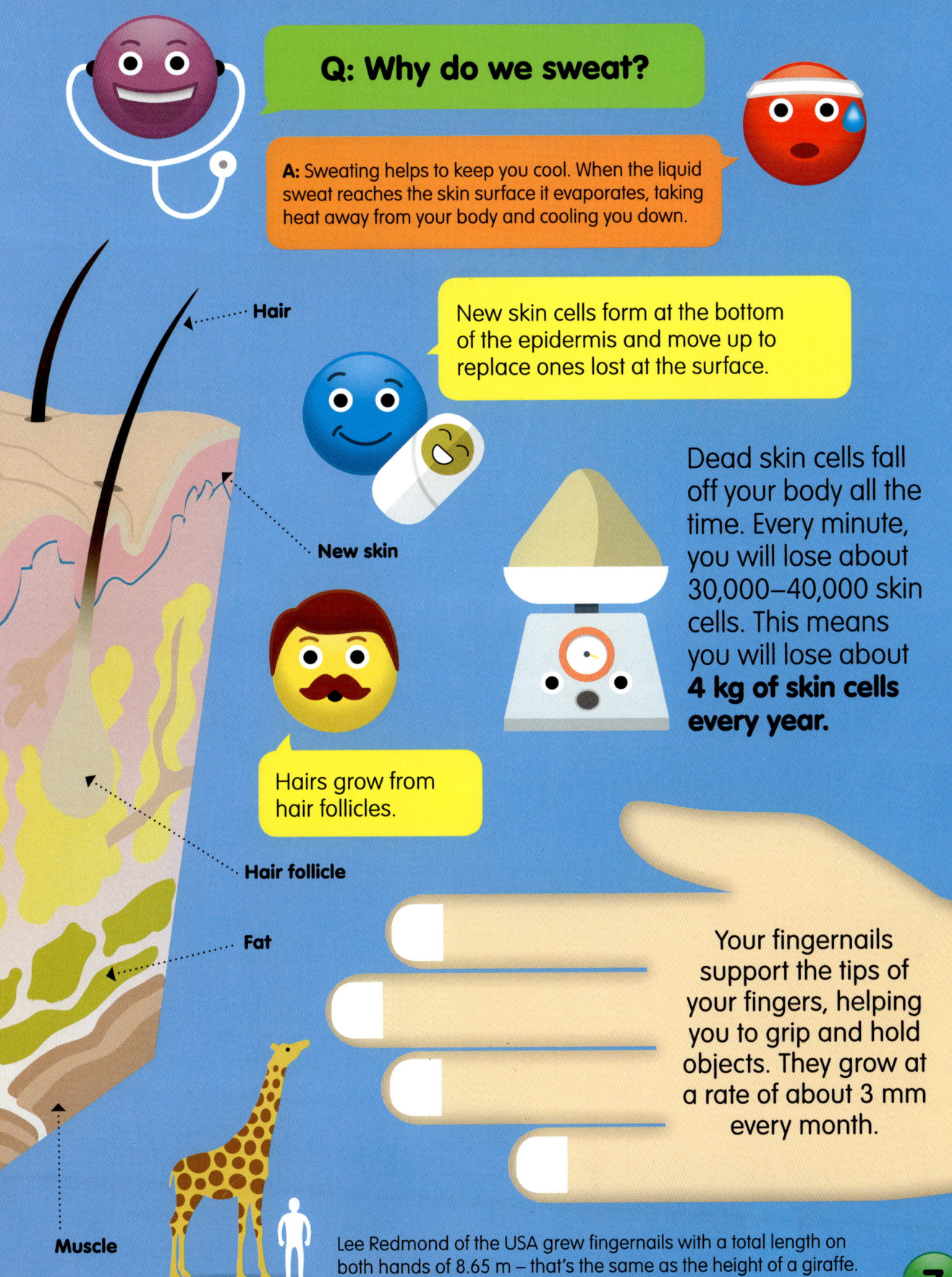

Q: Why do we sweat?

A: Sweating helps to keep you cool. When the liquid sweat reaches the skin surface it evaporates, taking heat away from your body and cooling you down.

New skin cells form at the bottom of the epidermis and move up to replace ones lost at the surface.

Hair

New skin

Dead skin cells fall off your body all the time. Every minute, you will lose about 30,000–40,000 skin cells. This means you will lose about **4 kg of skin cells every year.**

Hairs grow from hair follicles.

Hair follicle

Fat

Your fingernails support the tips of your fingers, helping you to grip and hold objects. They grow at a rate of about 3 mm every month.

Muscle

Lee Redmond of the USA grew fingernails with a total length on both hands of 8.65 m – that's the same as the height of a giraffe.

7

BONY BITS

Inside your body is a structure of super-tough rods, plates and other shapes made from strong bone tissue. These bones keep you in shape and help you to move around.

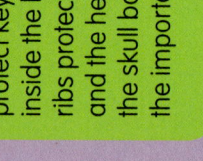

An adult human has **206 bones** in their skeleton. But a newborn baby has about **300 bones**. Some of these bones fuse together as the child grows up.

Protection
Some bones help to protect key organs inside the body. The ribs protect the lungs and the heart, while the skull bones protect the important brain.

More than **half the bones** in an adult's body are found in the feet, hands and wrists.

Flat bone

Irregular bone

Bone shapes
Bones come in different shapes depending on the jobs they do.

Flat bones include the skull bones, shoulder blades and ribs. They protect organs and act as attachment points for muscles.

Irregular bones have no set shape and include the vertebrae that make up your spine.

The places where bones meet are called joints.

Rigid
Some joints are rigid and provide little or no movement, such as the joints between the skull bones.

Other joints are designed for a lot of movement, so you can swing your limbs about freely.

Ouch! That hurt!

Sesamoid bone

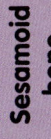

Short bone

Long bone

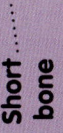

Short bones found in the foot and palm of the hand give a stable base for these parts.

Long bones found in the arms and legs help to move these long limbs.

Sesamoid bones are shaped like sesame seeds, and are usually found in joints, such as the knee, and help to protect tendons from high pressures.

Bones and joints that have become worn out, damaged, or even lost can be replaced by artificial body parts and even whole new limbs. These new body parts are made from composite materials, ceramics and metals so that they are lightweight and strong. Some can even be controlled by the wearer's thoughts.

MUSCLES AND MOVING

Muscle tissue has the amazing ability to contract, or get shorter. This means that it can pull on other body parts allowing you to move your limbs about or move things through your body.

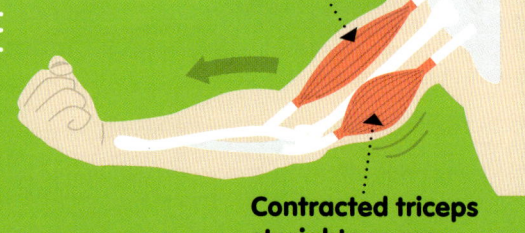

Contracted biceps bends arm

Muscles only work when they contract – they can only pull and cannot push. As such, they have to work in teams so that you can move body parts in lots of different directions.

Relaxed triceps

Relaxed biceps

Muscle tissue is made from two types of fibres. These fibres slide over each other to make the muscle shorter so it can pull on objects.

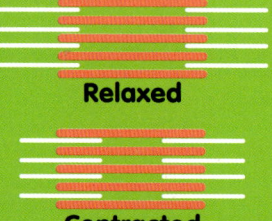

Relaxed

Contracted

Contracted triceps straightens arm

There are three types of muscle tissue:

Skeletal muscle is attached to your bones and helps you to move.

Smooth muscle tissue is found in different parts, such as your lungs, blood vessels and intestines. It carries out a number of jobs, such as pushing food through your guts.

Cardiac muscle is found in your heart. It pumps blood around your whole body.

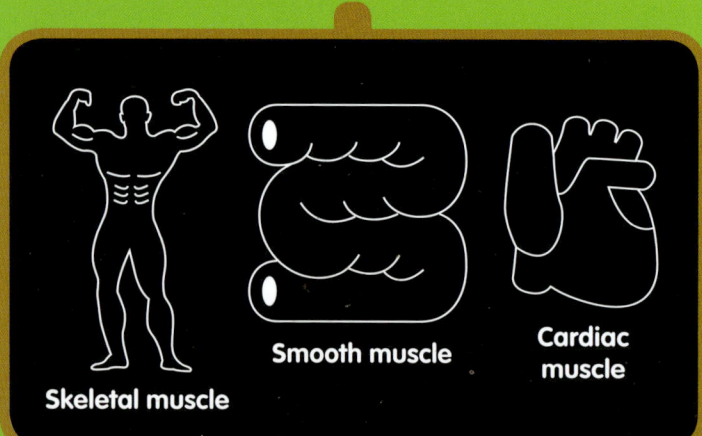

Skeletal muscle

Smooth muscle

Cardiac muscle

Your heart beats on average 80 times a minute, 4,800 times an hour, 115,200 times a day, 42,048,000 times a year.

If you live to 80, it will beat almost 3.5 billion times!

If you exercise soon after eating, blood is diverted from your intestines to your skeletal muscles. The intestines keep working to move and process the food, but they may not have enough oxygen, so they start to produce lactic acid. If too much of this lactic acid builds up, it causes cramps and a sharp pain, which is sometimes called a stitch.

This could take a while to take off!

It didn't look that heavy!

Kevin Fast of Canada set a world record for the heaviest aircraft pulled, when he dragged a CC-17 Globemaster weighing 188.83 tonnes a distance of 8.8 m.

EAT, CHEW, POO, REPEAT

Your body is just one big tube. Food is put into the mouth at one end. It is then pushed and processed through the long tube that makes up your intestines so that good stuff is taken out, leaving unwanted stuff to get rid of.

Chew time
Your teeth have different shapes depending on the job they do.

Incisors are flat and thin to chop off bits of food.

Molars and premolars are large and flat to grind up food.

Canines are sharp and pointed to grasp and hold food.

Balanced diet

Protein 55 g, **Carbohydrates** 300 g, **Sugar** 120 g, **Fat** 95 g, **Saturates** 30 g, **Salt** 6 g

Men
2,500 kilocalories

Protein 50 g, **Carbohydrates** 260 g, **Sugar** 90 g, **Fat** 70 g, **Saturates** 20 g, **Salt** 6 g

Women
2,000 kilocalories

Time through the tube

Mouth and oesophagus
1–10 seconds

Stomach
3 hours

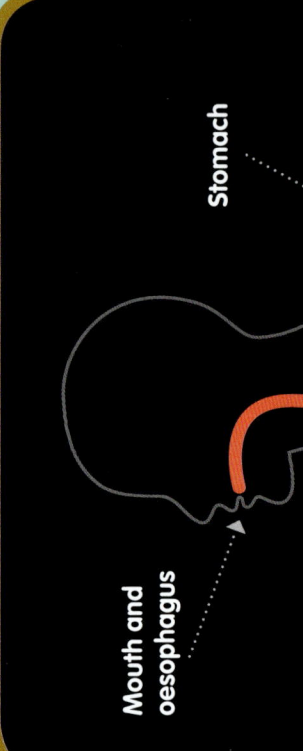

Mouth and oesophagus

Stomach

An adult will produce about 100–250 grams of poo every day.

Large intestine **11–16 hours**

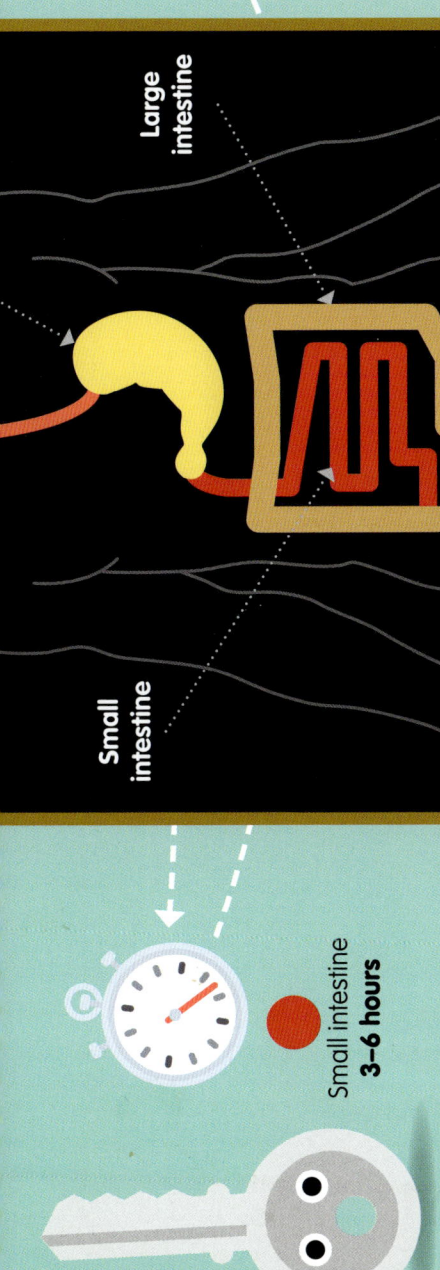

Large intestine

Small intestine

Rectum

Poo is made up of:

75% water

25% solid matter ...

... of which **30%** is dead bacteria, **30%** indigestible food, **10–20%** cholesterol, **10–20%** inorganic matter such as calcium phosphate and iron phosphate, **2–3%** protein.

Poo
At the end of its journey, your body gets rid of the unwanted material as poo.

Rectum **up to 48 hours**

Small intestine **3–6 hours**

Lock and key
As food travels through your body, different parts of it are chopped up by special chemicals called enzymes. These attach themselves to a specific part of the food, like a key in a lock, and split the food apart.

IN A HEARTBEAT

Running through your body is a network of tubes. These carry blood to every single cell and, with it, the oxygen and nutrients these cells need to survive. The blood also carries away any unwanted waste substances.

The heart is divided into two halves, and each half has two chambers: an upper atrium and a lower ventricle.

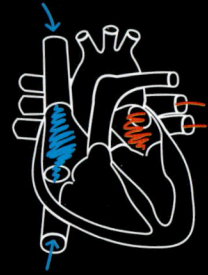

Blood enters the two atria from large veins.

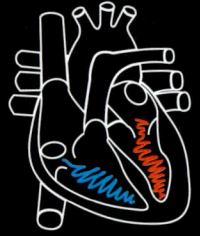

The valves at the bottom of the atria open and the muscles around the atria contract to push the blood down into the ventricles.

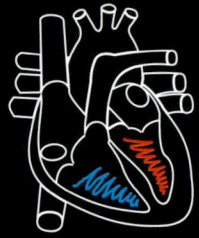

The valves between the atria and the ventricles then snap shut.

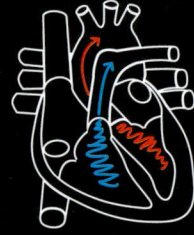

The muscles around the ventricles then contract to push the blood out of the heart and into the arteries.

There are three types of blood vessel:

Veins carry blood back to the heart.

Arteries carry blood away from the heart.

Capillaries are tiny blood vessels where gases and nutrients are transferred to and from the blood.

How much blood?

An average adult has about 5 litres of blood.

With each beat

Your heart pumps about 70 ml of blood around the body – about the same volume as a chicken's egg.

Every minute

Your heart will pump 5 litres of blood around the body – about half the volume of a basketball.

In an hour

It will pump about 300 litres – enough to nearly fill two bath tubs.

In a year

Your heart will have pumped enough blood to fill an Olympic-sized swimming pool – 2.5 million litres.

What's in blood?

- **55 per cent** of blood is a straw-coloured liquid called plasma.

- **Almost 45 per cent** of blood is made up of red blood cells.

- **Less than 1 per cent** is made up of white blood cells and platelets.

In 1628, I published a book where I put forward the idea that blood circulated around the body and was pumped by the heart. Before then, scientists thought the lungs moved blood around and that it was absorbed by the body's tissues.

WILLIAM HARVEY

15

FIGHTING INVADERS

Every minute of every day, your body is fighting off invasion from foreign objects. Fortunately, your body has an array of powerful defences it can unleash against these attackers.

On the outside
Your skin provides a tough water-resistant barrier against invasion. The tough skin cells form a physical barrier, and they are covered by an oily substance called sebum to put off nasty bugs. It's also home to lots of harmless bacteria that stop harmful ones multiplying out of control.

Grrrrr

Yum, yum!
The white blood cells in your blood play a key part in the fight against disease.

Some of us will surround and engulf foreign objects, including bacteria, and eat them!

Antibiotics
Sir Alexander Fleming made a discovery that revolutionised medicine – by accident! Returning to his laboratory after a weekend away, he found that some dishes in which he had been growing bacteria had been infected by a mould that destroyed the bacteria. The mould was penicillin, the first antibiotic, and it has gone on to save millions of lives.

White blood cell

Bacteria

White blood cell surrounds bacteria

Bacteria is broken down

Debris released by blood cell

Edward Jenner and vaccines
At the end of the 18th century, English scientist Edward Jenner developed the first vaccine. He noted that people infected with cowpox, a mild disease, were immune from smallpox. He injected people with doses of cowpox to protect them from deadly smallpox.

EDWARD JENNER

Putting up a fight
Sometimes, your body's defence mechanisms can cause problems:

A sensitivity to plant seeds can produce an allergic reaction and the runny nose and sneezing that we call hay fever.

Doctors and surgeons need to be very careful with blood transfusions and transplants. The blood type must match that of the patient. There are four main blood types: O, A, B and AB.

The receiver's body may start to attack a transplant, causing it to reject the replacement body part.

Type O is the universal donor

Donor

O

Receiver

A

B

AB

A

B

AB

Donor

Receiver

BREATHE IN, BREATHE OUT

You are surrounded by stuff that is vital to your existence – oxygen. But just how do you get this colourless and odourless gas inside your body and to where it's most needed?

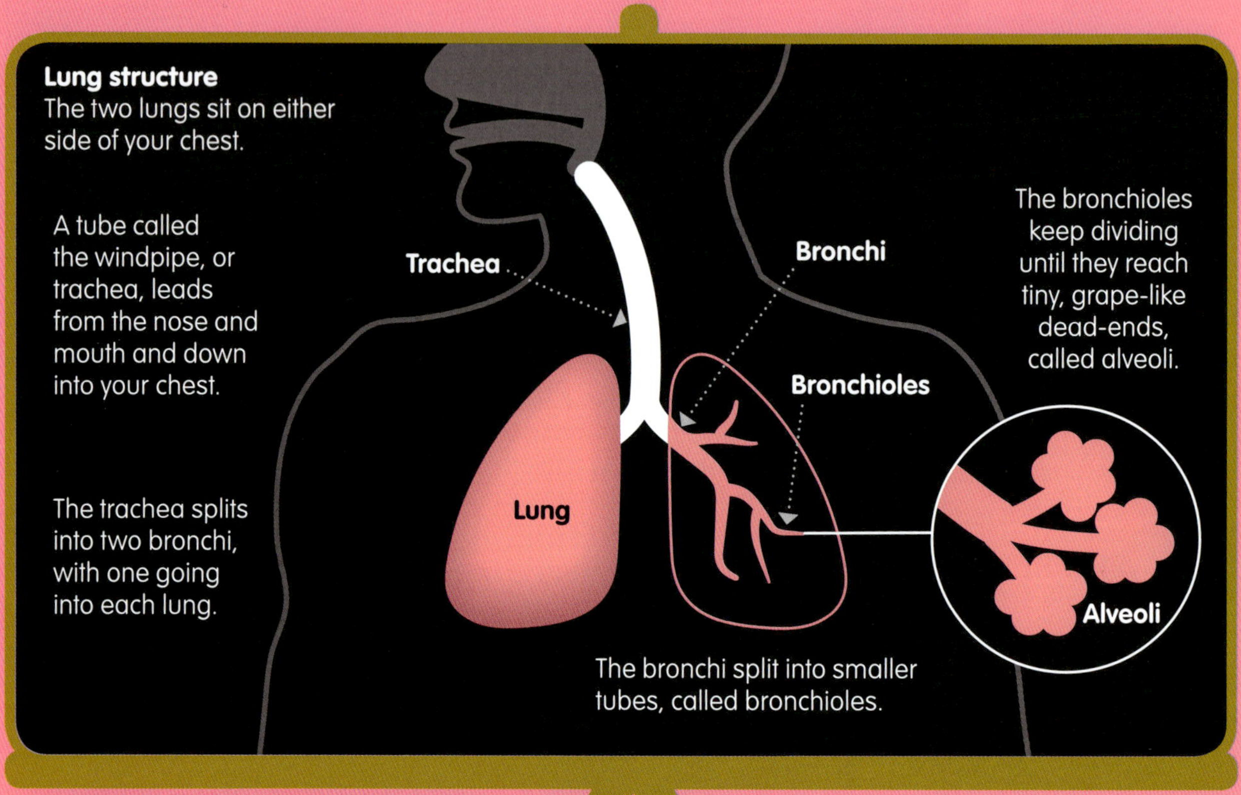

Lung structure
The two lungs sit on either side of your chest.

A tube called the windpipe, or trachea, leads from the nose and mouth and down into your chest.

The trachea splits into two bronchi, with one going into each lung.

Trachea

Lung

Bronchi

Bronchioles

The bronchioles keep dividing until they reach tiny, grape-like dead-ends, called alveoli.

Alveoli

The bronchi split into smaller tubes, called bronchioles.

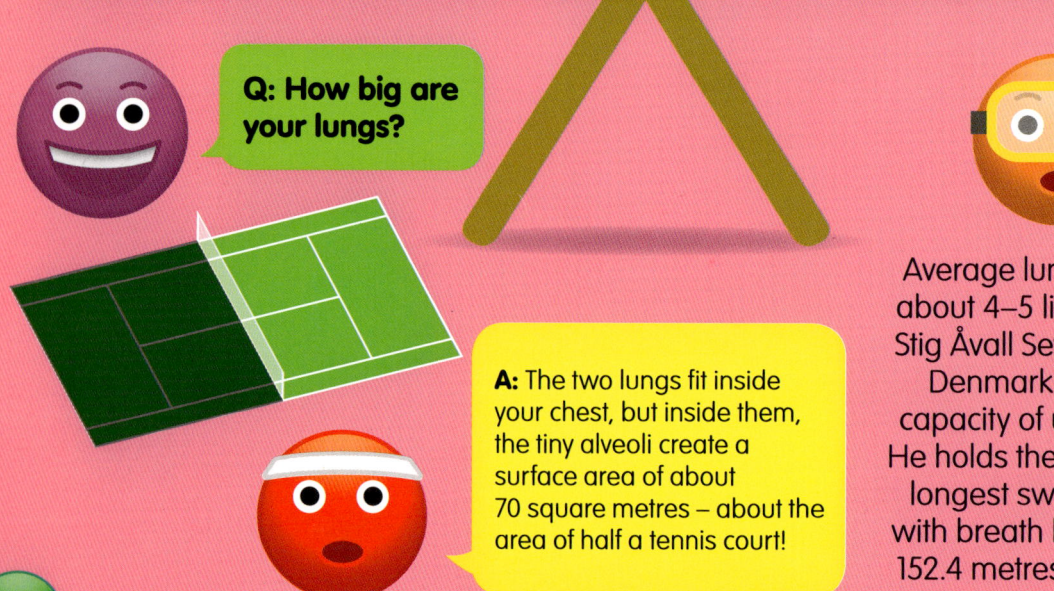

Q: How big are your lungs?

A: The two lungs fit inside your chest, but inside them, the tiny alveoli create a surface area of about 70 square metres – about the area of half a tennis court!

Average lung capacity is about 4–5 litres of air, but Stig Åvall Severinsen from Denmark has a lung capacity of up to 14 litres. He holds the record for the longest swim under ice with breath held, covering 152.4 metres underwater.

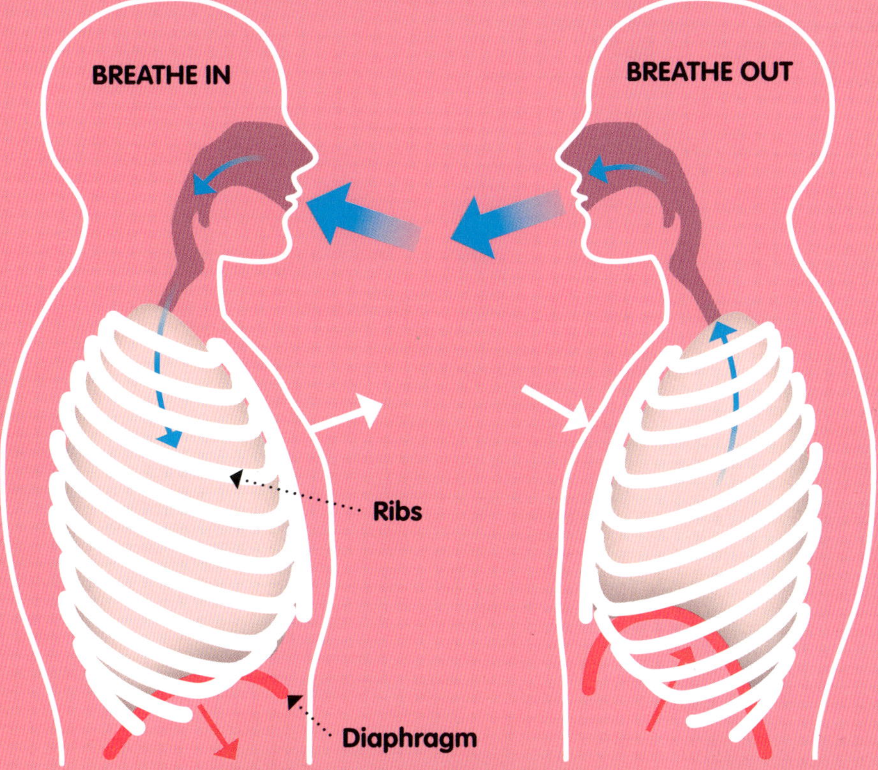

BREATHE IN

BREATHE OUT

Ribs

Diaphragm

A person will breathe about 11,000 litres of air every day ...

... that's enough to fill more than 70 bathtubs.

To breathe in, muscles between the ribs contract to lift the whole ribcage. At the same time, a sheet of muscle beneath the lungs, called the diaphragm, flattens. Together, these expand the lungs so that air is pushed in through the nose and mouth and down into the lungs.

To breathe out, the diaphragm relaxes and domes up, while the muscles between the ribs relax so that the ribcage falls. This pushes on the lungs to squeeze air out of them.

Inside the lungs, oxygen moves from the air and into the blood. At the same time, waste carbon dioxide moves out of the blood and into the air to be breathed out.

When resting, you will breathe about 15 times each minute.

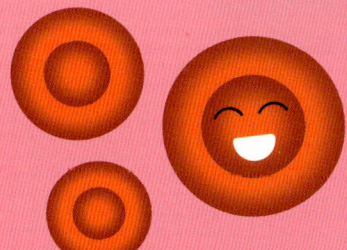

When you are exercising, you will breathe about 80 times a minute.

19

WASTE CONTROL

Located on either side of your back are two small organs called kidneys. These play a key role in filtering your blood and cleaning it of any waste products your body produces as it goes about its business. They also help to balance the water levels in your body.

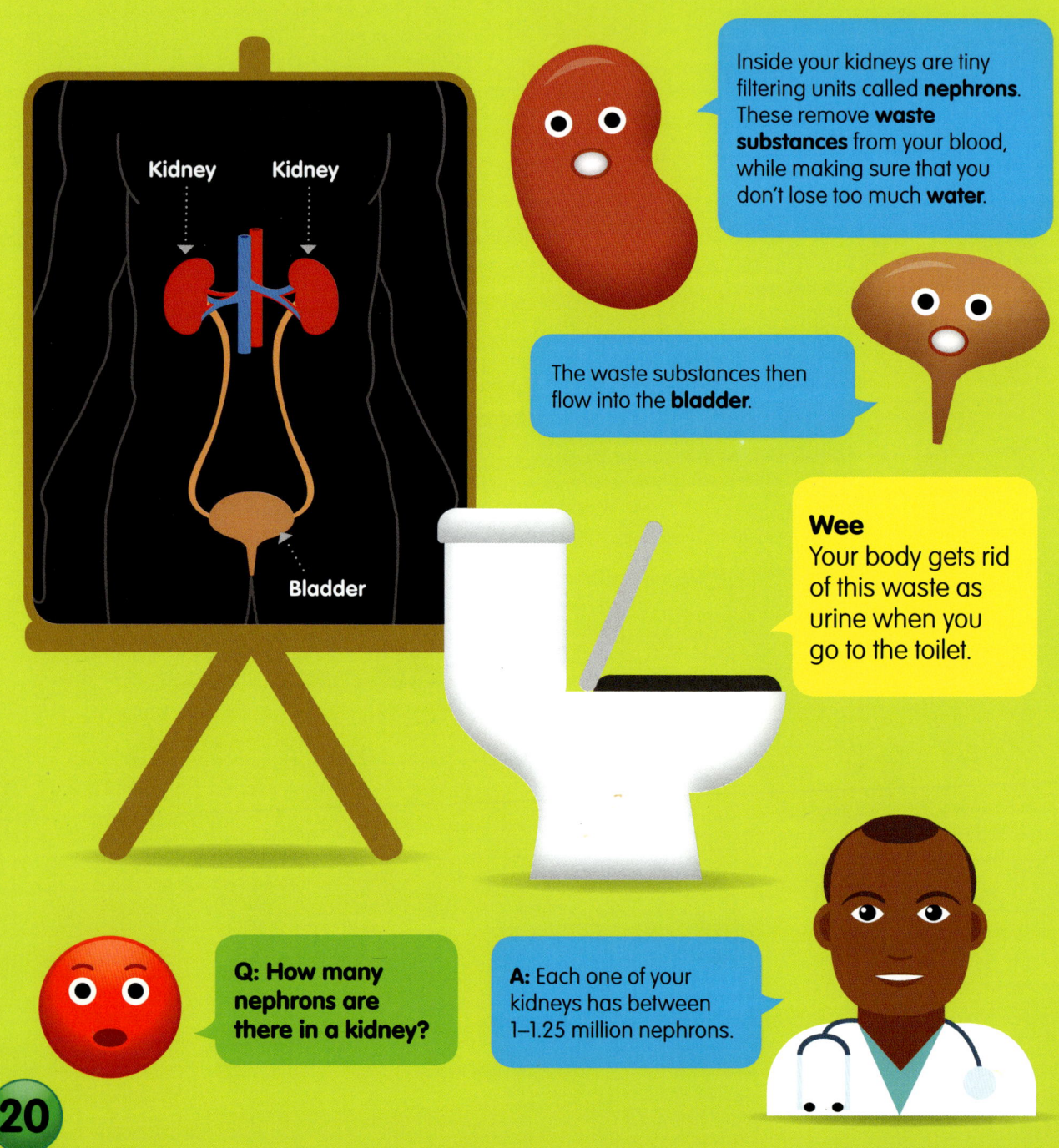

Kidney   Kidney

Bladder

Inside your kidneys are tiny filtering units called **nephrons**. These remove **waste substances** from your blood, while making sure that you don't lose too much **water**.

The waste substances then flow into the **bladder**.

Wee
Your body gets rid of this waste as urine when you go to the toilet.

Q: How many nephrons are there in a kidney?

A: Each one of your kidneys has between 1–1.25 million nephrons.

Water balance

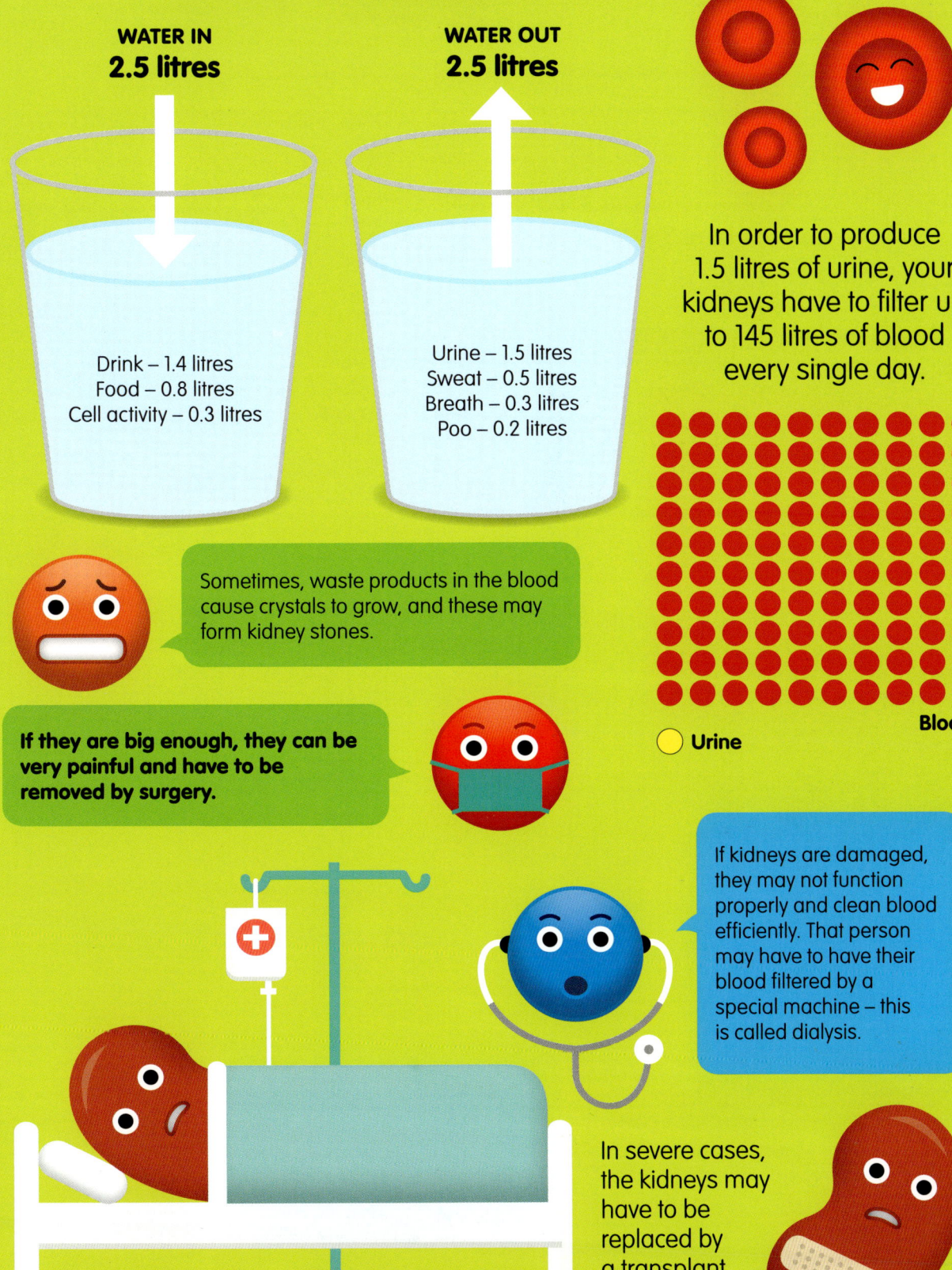

WATER IN
2.5 litres

Drink – 1.4 litres
Food – 0.8 litres
Cell activity – 0.3 litres

WATER OUT
2.5 litres

Urine – 1.5 litres
Sweat – 0.5 litres
Breath – 0.3 litres
Poo – 0.2 litres

In order to produce 1.5 litres of urine, your kidneys have to filter up to 145 litres of blood every single day.

○ **Urine**   **Blood**

Sometimes, waste products in the blood cause crystals to grow, and these may form kidney stones.

If they are big enough, they can be very painful and have to be removed by surgery.

If kidneys are damaged, they may not function properly and clean blood efficiently. That person may have to have their blood filtered by a special machine – this is called dialysis.

In severe cases, the kidneys may have to be replaced by a transplant.

SENDING SIGNALS

Your body contains a vast network of tiny 'wires', called nerves. These carry signals to and from your body's control centre, the brain. They supply information about how your body is performing and the world around you, as well as instructions telling different body parts how to behave.

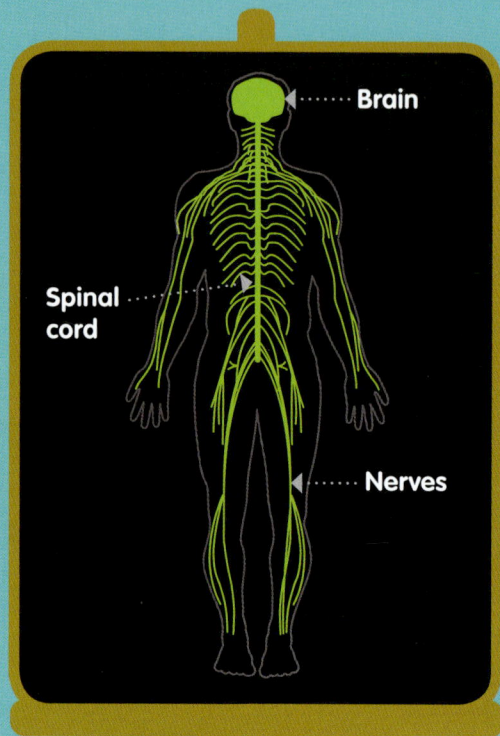

Brain

Spinal cord

Nerves

The nervous system
Your brain sits inside your head. The spinal cord runs from the bottom of the brain and down to your … bottom!

Riding the wave
Signals are sent along the nerves by pumping sodium and potassium ions into and out of them, to create a moving electric charge, like a wave.

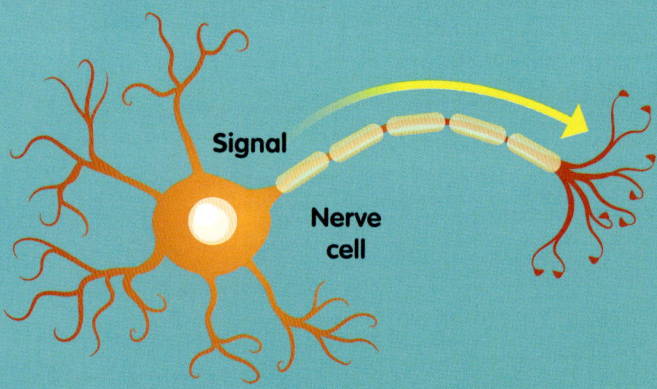

Signal

Nerve cell

Q: How fast can nerve signals travel?

A: Nerve signals travel at up to 300 kph, about the speed of a supercar – it takes just 0.02 seconds for a signal to travel from your foot to your brain!

Mind the gap!

Nerve signals travel from one nerve cell to another across a tiny gap called a synapse. The nerve cell carrying the signal releases special chemical messengers that diffuse across the synapse and bind with the next nerve cell to continue the signal.

At any one time, only 4 per cent of your brain's cells are active, while the rest are kept in reserve. Zzzzzz

Your brain contains about 100 billion nerve cells – that's more than there are stars in the Milky Way galaxy!

Your brain makes up just **2 per cent** of your body weight …

… but it uses about **20 per cent** of your body's total energy needs.

20%

Reflex

Many of your body's actions occur without you thinking. Some of these are reflex reactions and they include your pupils changing size to match different light conditions.

Bright

pupil

Dark

SUPER SENSES

Your body contains millions of sensory receptors, which collect and send information from the world around you and your body, and pass them on to your brain to interpret. These signals can be touch, sight, sound, smell and taste.

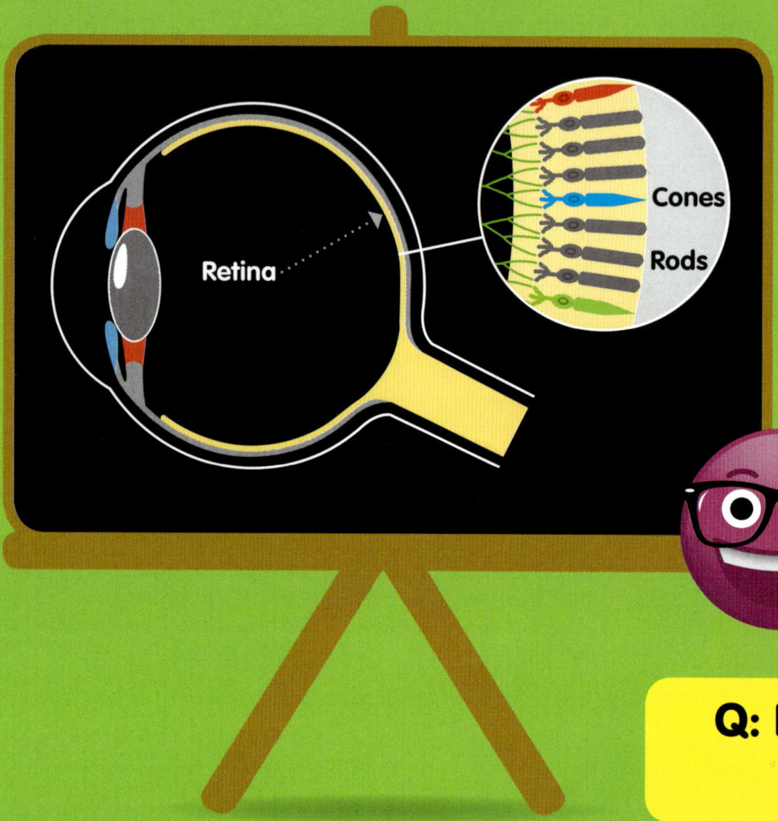

Retina

Cones

Rods

The back of the eye, called the retina, is covered with two types of light-sensitive cell, called photoreceptors. There are about 130 million rod-shaped cells that are sensitive to low levels of light, but do not detect colour. There are about 7 million cone-shaped cells that detect colours.

Q: How many colours can we see?

A: Usually, humans can detect up to ten million different colours. Some people with very sensitive vision, called tetrachromats, can detect about 100 million colours.

Ear, ear!
Each of your ears contains the three smallest bones in your body: the malleus, stapes and incus. Together, these bones are called the ossicles. They transmit and amplify sound waves to your eardrum.

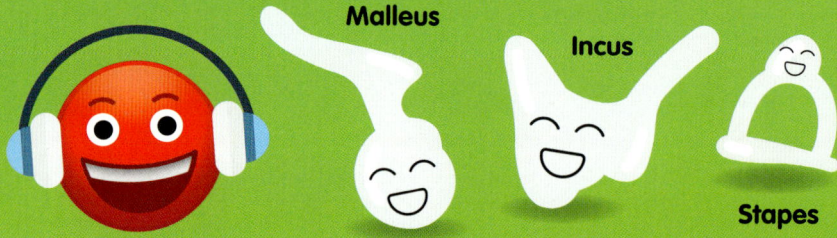

Malleus

Incus

Stapes

A matter of taste
Your tongue and other parts of your mouth have special cells called taste buds. These detect five different types of flavour, which are sweet, sour, bitter, salty and umami (savoury).

Sweet

Umami

Sour

Bitter

Salty

Smell
A human has about **5-6 million** odour-detecting cells. Rabbits have about **100 million**, while dogs have **220 million**.

Touch
Different parts of your body are more sensitive than others. Scientists use the two-point test to see how sensitive different body parts are – it tests how far apart two points have to be for both points to be detected.

TONGUE
1.1 mm

FINGERS
3 mm

BACK
up to 75 mm

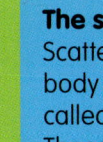

The sixth sense?
Scattered around your body are special sensors called proprioceptors. These send signals back to your brain about the position of your body parts and what they are up to.

Not sure I like this balancing act!

In balance
Inside each of your ears are three round tubes, called the semicircular canals. They tell you which way up your body is and help you to stay balanced.

CHEMICAL MESSENGERS

There are several organs located around your body that produce a number of special chemicals called hormones. These chemicals tell parts of your body how to behave.

Bedtime
The pineal gland at the base of your brain makes a hormone called melatonin. This makes you feel sleepy when it is time for bed.

Thyroid
This butterfly-shaped gland in your neck produces the hormone calcitonin, which controls how much calcium is in your blood.

... it also releases a hormone which controls how much water your kidneys absorb back into your blood.

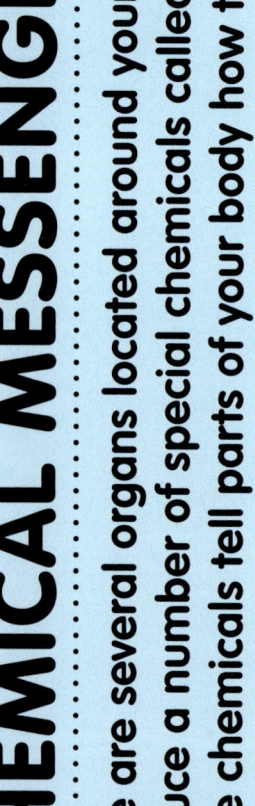

Growing up
The pituitary gland is found at the base of your brain and produces several hormones, including growth hormone, which controls how fast and how much you grow ...

Pain control
Your brain produces hormones, such as endorphins, that act as natural painkillers.

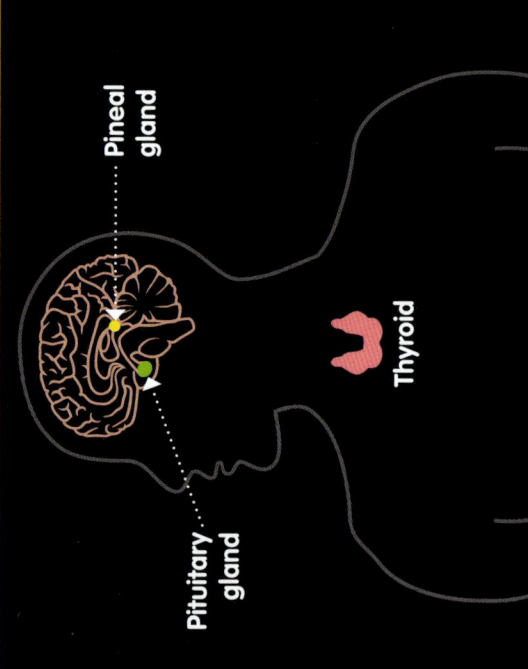

Pineal gland

Pituitary gland

Thyroid

Balancing sugars

Your pancreas makes hormones, such as insulin, that control the amount of sugar in your blood. If the pancreas stops working properly, it can lead to a condition called diabetes.

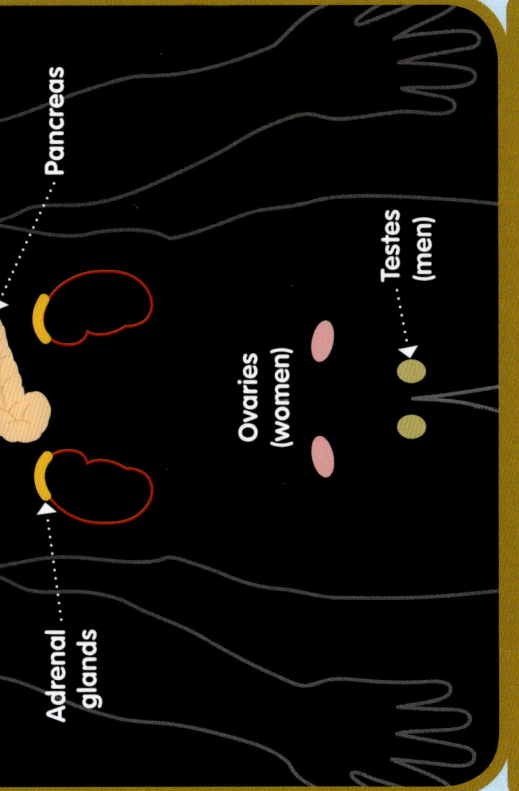

Pancreas

Adrenal glands

Ovaries (women)

Testes (men)

Hormone facts:
Robert Wadlow was the tallest person ever. He grew to a height of 2.72 metres and his shoes were a size 37AA (47 cm long).

Average man

Robert Wadlow

Fight or flight

The adrenal glands sit on top of each of your kidneys and they produce the hormone adrenaline. In a stressful situation, this increases your heart rate, makes the pupils in your eyes bigger and increases the size of some of your blood vessels. All of this prepares your body to confront the stressful situation, or to run away.

Sex hormones

These are produced by the ovaries in women and the testes in men. The ovaries produce hormones that control the release of eggs, while hormones produced by the testes control the rate at which sperm is produced.

Sperm

Egg

27

REPRODUCTION AND GROWING UP

A new life begins when a male sex cell fuses with a female sex cell. These fused cells form a new, complete cell which starts to divide and grow, becoming a developing infant in the womb of the mother. After nine months, the infant is born and then starts its long journey towards old age.

In Vitro Fertilisation (IVF) is the process where sperm and egg are fused outside of the womb.

Size in the womb ...

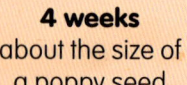

Fertilisation
about 120 micrometres across

4 weeks
about the size of a poppy seed

6 weeks
about the size of a lentil

8 weeks
about the size of a kidney bean

14 weeks
about the size of a lemon

23 weeks
about the size of a large mango

During the first year of its life, an infant may grow about 25 centimetres in length **and triple its weight.**

After the age of two, growth may continue at a rate of about 6 cm a year.

The ageing body

As you get older, you may find that your body isn't able to do what it could at its peak.

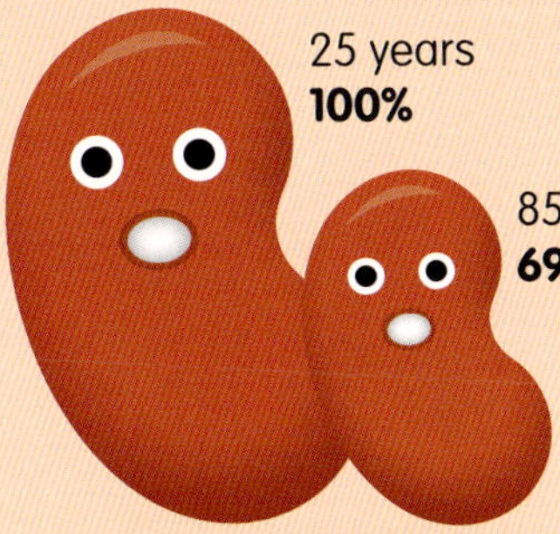

Kidney function 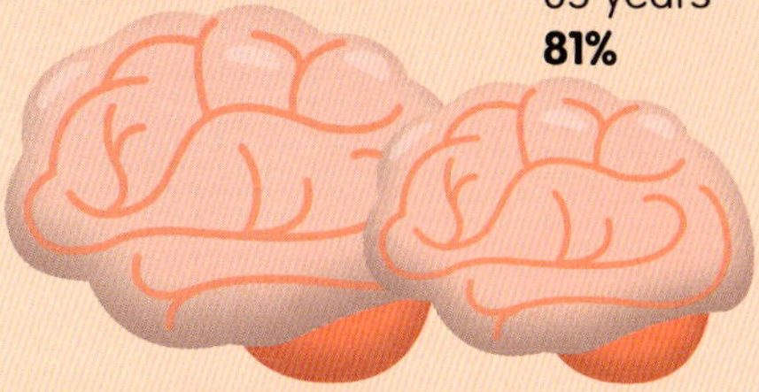
25 years **100%**
85 years **69%**

Brain function 
25 years **100%**
85 years **81%**

Muscle strength 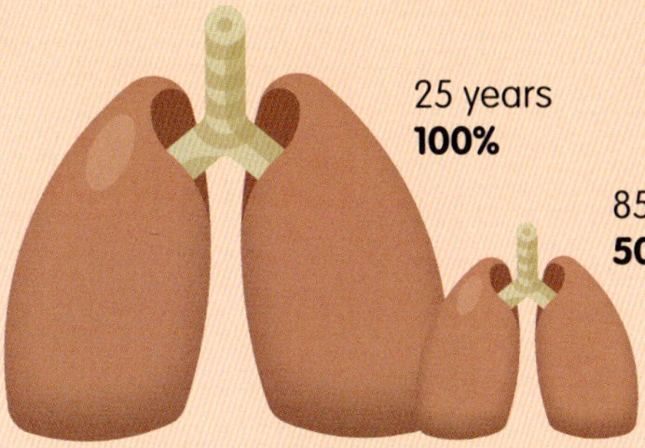
25 years **100%**
85 years **55%**

Lung capacity
25 years **100%**
85 years **50%**

It's getting cramped in here!

30 weeks
about the size of a cabbage

39 weeks
about the size of a small watermelon

Oldest Ever
The oldest person ever was Jeanne Calment of France who lived to the age of 122 years and 164 days.

GLOSSARY

ALLERGIC REACTION
When the body's immune system is very sensitive to a substance, such as plant pollen, and overreacts. Symptoms can include a runny nose, a rash and the swelling of body parts.

ALVEOLI
The tiny, hollow, grape-shaped structures where gas exchange takes place inside the lungs.

ANTIBIOTICS
A type of medicine used to kill bacteria and fight infections.

ARTERIES
The thick, muscular blood vessels that carry blood away from the heart under high pressure.

ATRIA
The two upper chambers of the heart.

BACTERIA
A tiny organism, usually made up of one cell, which can cause disease.

BLADDER
The stretchable sac where urine is stored before it leaves your body.

BRONCHI
The branches of the airways that enter each of the lungs.

BRONCHIOLES
The smaller airways that branch off from the bronchi inside the lungs.

CAPILLARIES
The very thin blood vessels that link the arteries and the veins and carry blood to the body's cells.

CELL
The tiny parts that make up living things and perform all the basic requirements for life.

DERMIS
The second layer of the skin, found below the epidermis. It contains the blood vessels and most of the touch sense receptors.

DIALYSIS
The artificial filtering of blood to clean it of waste material.

DIAPHRAGM
The thin sheet of muscle that sits in a dome shape below the lungs.

EPIDERMIS
The top layer of skin.

HORMONES
Chemicals that are produced by various glands around your body, which tell other body parts how to function and behave.

JOINTS

The parts where two bones meet. Joints can be rigid, like the joints in your skull, or flexible, such as your knee joints.

LUNG CAPACITY

The volume of air that your lungs can hold.

NEPHRONS

The tiny filtering units that are found in your kidneys and which filter and clean your blood.

OESOPHAGUS

The tube that links the back of your throat and your stomach.

ORGAN

A part of your body that is made up of a number of tissues and which carries out a specific function, such as your brain or your lungs.

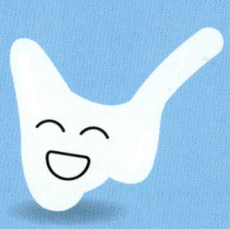

OSSICLES

The name for the tiny bones in your ears, which transmit sound waves to the eardrum.

PHOTORECEPTORS

The light-sensitive cells that line the retina at the back of your eyeballs.

PLASMA

The straw-coloured liquid that supports the blood cells.

PLATELETS

A small type of blood cell that plays an important part in clotting blood and stopping bleeding during an injury.

PROPRIOCEPTORS

Sensors around the body that supply information about the angle of joints, position of limbs and the performance of muscles.

RED BLOOD CELLS

Doughnut-shaped blood cells that carry oxygen to the body's cells and carbon dioxide away.

SEBUM

An oily substance that is produced by glands in your skin.

SYNAPSE

The gap between nerve cells, across which a nerve signal must pass.

TRANSFUSION

Taking blood that has come from one person and giving it to another person.

WHITE BLOOD CELLS

Various large types of blood cell that carry out important roles in fighting disease and infection.

INDEX